CALLING ALL INNOVATORS
A CAREER FOR YOU

TOYS
FROM CONCEPT TO CONSUMER

BY KEVIN CUNNINGHAM

CHILDREN'S PRESS®
An Imprint of Scholastic Inc.
New York Toronto London Auckland Sydney
Mexico City New Delhi Hong Kong
Danbury, Connecticut

CONTENT CONSULTANT
Nate Lau, Toy Designer, Tegu

PHOTOGRAPHS © 2014: Alamy Images: 15 top (Chris Willson), 24 left (Design Pics Inc.),
53 (DWImages), 7 (Finnbarr Webster), 17 (Gunter Nezhoda), 10 (H. Mark Weidman
Photography), 54 bottom (Image Source), 14 right (INTERFOTO), 41 left (Jeff Greenberg
"0 people images"), 15 bottom (Paul Carter), 12 top (Robin Beckham/BEEPstock), 13,
29 bottom (ZUMA Press, Inc.); AP Images: 12 bottom (Cheryl Gerber for Mattel), 50 (Court
Mast/Yahoo!), 2 (Craig Ruttle), 34 (Gene Kaiser/South Bend Tribune), 16 left (Jason
DeCrow/Invision for Hasbro), 27, 61 (Mark Lennihan), 9 (Matt Rourke), 39 (Michael
S. Wirtz/The Philadelphia Inquirer), 59 (Press Association), 28 top, 29 top, 4 right, 26
(PRNewsFoto/Activision Publishing, Inc.), 23, 58 (Rex Features), 44 (Sebastian Widmann/
dapd), 46 (SIMON ISABELLE/SIPA), 51 (Sipa); Corbis Images/Lego: 14 left; Dr. Barry
Kudrowitz: 48, 49 top, 49 bottom; Dreamstime/Rigmanyi: 55 left; Getty Images/Dorling
Kindersley : 4 left, 8; iStockphoto/Tom Brown: 28 bottom; Media Bakery: 20, 24 right, 25
top, 38, 54 top; Courtesy of Nate Lau: 36 bottom, 36 top, 37, 55 right; Nathan Sawaya,
Inc./www.brickartist.com: cover, 3; Newscom: 19 (CB2/ZOB/WENN), 42 (David Toerge/
BlackStar Photos), 30 (KENNELL KRISTA/SIPA), 57 (Lu Hanxin/Xinhua/Photoshot), 22 (MBR
KRT), 31 (Ross Hailey/MCT), 16 right (Splash News); PhotoEdit: 40 (Annette Udvardi), 18
(Cindy Charles), 5 right, 47 (David Young-Wolff), 5 left, 41 right (Michelle D. Bridwell), 25
bottom (Richard Hutchings); Superstock, Inc.: 52 (Asia Images), 6 (DeAgostini); Thinkstock/
iStockphoto: 56; Zuma Press/Tan Jin/Xinhua: 35.

LIBRARY OF CONGRESS CATALOGING-IN-PUBLICATION DATA
  Toys : from concept to consumer / by Kevin Cunningham.
      pages cm. — (Calling all innovators, a career for you)
  Audience: 9–12.
  Audience: Grade 4 to 6.
  Includes bibliographical references and index.
  ISBN 978-0-531-26522-2 (lib. bdg.) — ISBN 978-0-531-22010-8 (pbk.)
  1. Toys—Design and construction—History—Juvenile literature. I. Title.
  TS2301.T7C754 2013
  688.7'2—dc23   2012034207

1 2 3 4 5 6 7 8 9 10 R 23 22 21 20 19 18 17 16 15 14

Science, technology, engineering, arts, and math are the fields that drive innovation. Whether they are finding ways to make our lives easier or developing the latest entertainment, the people who work in these fields are changing the world for the better. Do you have what it takes to join the ranks of today's greatest innovators? Read on to discover whether toy design is a career for you.

TABLE *of* CONTENTS

In the past, wooden dolls and other toys were often homemade.

LeapPad is a top-selling toy because it offers kids a variety of fun and educational activities.

When it comes to selling big in the toy industry, a toy's packaging is almost as important as the toy itself.

A prototype is one of the first steps in the production of a toy.

This toy was discovered in the ancient ruins of Mohenjo-daro, in what is now Pakistan.

CHAPTER ONE

PLAYING IN THE PAST

From kids spending entire afternoons building cities out of colored blocks, to adults collecting their favorite action figures and competing at board games, almost everyone enjoys toys. Whether you're into the robots, video games, and other technological marvels that are all around today, or your toy box is filled with more traditional action figures, dolls, **die-cast** cars, and blocks, you have probably enjoyed countless hours of fun playing with your favorite toys.

People have been making and playing with toys for thousands of years. The ancient Greeks made dolls, while the ancient Chinese are famous for their beautiful kites and wooden puzzle toys. The wheeled, animal-shaped toys of Central America's ancient Olmec people are not all that different from today's toy cars and trucks. Just as they do today, toys kept kids busy in ancient civilizations while teaching them important life skills and encouraging creativity.

20TH-CENTURY TRIUMPHS

1902	1949	1952	1964
The first teddy bears are sold.	The first Lego bricks are released.	Mr. Potato Head becomes one of the most popular vinyl plastic toys.	Mattel releases G.I. Joe, the first action figure.

INDUSTRIAL INNOVATIONS

Toys have existed since ancient times, but kids in the past did not always have as much time to play as they often do now. Instead, they had many household chores and often worked jobs to help support their families. In colonial America, many children did not even have time for school. Instead, they learned valuable skills during the small amounts of free time they had playing with homemade toys. Wooden animal figures helped teach about farming, while simple rag dolls gave young girls practice in raising children. Other popular toys of the time included spinning tops, wooden soldiers, whistles, and drums.

In the early 1800s, people began to buy factory-made toys and gradually stopped making their own. Factories could easily make metal toys, which soon became more popular than wooden ones. Metal roller skates were a hit in the late 1800s. Tin soldiers and animals were also popular.

PAPIER-MÂCHÉ HEAD

HANDMADE CLOTHING

WOODEN LEGS

PAINTED SHOES

Dolls were once made mainly of wood and dressed in handmade clothing.

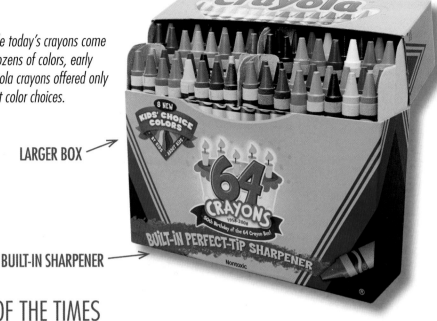

While today's crayons come in dozens of colors, early Crayola crayons offered only eight color choices.

LARGER BOX →

BUILT-IN SHARPENER →

TOYS OF THE TIMES

The toy business was interrupted when the U.S. government needed metal, rubber, and other materials to make supplies for troops during the Civil War (1861–1865). After the war, new toys reflected a widespread fascination with machines. Iron train models became popular as real-life railroads sprang up across the nation, and the invention of the automobile and the airplane made toy cars and planes a must-have gift.

But two of the most iconic toys of the following decades had nothing to do with machines. In 1902, a newspaper cartoon about new president Theodore "Teddy" Roosevelt inspired Brooklyn shop owners Morris and Rose Michtom to make and sell a stuffed bear. Their teddy bear, named after the president, became an instant best seller. Soon, dozens of companies jumped into the teddy bear business. Bears from Winnie the Pooh to Paddington have stayed on toy shelves ever since. Another toy legend got its start the next year, when Crayola's original box of eight colored crayons arrived in stores. Though crayons had existed in some form for hundreds of years, it was Crayola that brought them true popularity as art toys.

FIRST THINGS FIRST

TECHNICIAN

CONTROL PANEL

COMPLETED PIECES

Plastic molds made it easier for toy makers to create large numbers of identical toys.

PLASTIC'S PROGRESS

It's hard to imagine a time when most toys and other household items were made out of metal or wood. Today, it is far more common for such things to be made from plastic. Plastic is an inexpensive substance that can easily be **molded** into almost any shape. Its rise in popularity during the 20th century made it an important part of many of the world's most popular toys.

EARLY RESISTANCE

The first widely used plastic, **celluloid**, appeared in 1869. Unfortunately, celluloid easily caught on fire—a major safety hazard. In addition, this plastic seemed cheap and flimsy compared to wood or metal. It took sturdier kinds of plastics, lower prices, and good advertising to convince consumers that plastic toys were a good idea.

George Lerner's Mr. Potato Head doll became one of the most popular vinyl toys when it hit stores in 1952. Children built the potato-shaped character's face using a variety of removable plastic eyes, ears, and other features.

SHAPES AND SIZES

In 1872, the brothers John and Isaiah Hyatt put plastic to use with a process called injection molding. In injection molding, tiny pieces of plastic pass through a tube. Inside the tube, heat softens the raw plastic. The machine then presses the melted plastic goo into a specially shaped mold to form buttons, combs, or other items.

SAFETY FIRST

A safer, tougher plastic called **vinyl** replaced celluloid in most products by the 1950s, bringing a new generation of toys. ☀

Later versions of Mr. Potato Head took advantage of new types of plastic.

ALL DOLLED UP

With the rise of plastic, by the mid-20th century toy inventors were free to let their imaginations run wild. A variety of plastic dolls shaped like babies and young girls were among the best-selling toys of the time. Many of the dolls had special features to help set them apart from competitors. Mattel's Chatty Cathy doll had a small record player inside her. Pull a string, and she said one of 11 phrases on the record. Other popular dolls cried or wet their diapers like real babies.

In 1959, Mattel released a new doll named Barbie. Unlike most other dolls of the time, she had the body of an adult woman instead of a baby. Barbie was an immediate hit. Mattel quickly began releasing a variety of Barbie products, including outfits, cars, and a boyfriend named Ken.

The original Barbie doll is not much different from the ones sold today.

RUTH HANDLER

Barbie was created by Ruth Handler, who cofounded Mattel along with her husband. When Handler first pitched the doll to her husband and the rest of Mattel's executive board, her idea was rejected. Handler persisted and eventually convinced them to produce the doll. Barbie became one of the most popular toys of all time, and Handler went on to become Mattel's president.

Ultimate Frisbee is a popular game in which teams compete to score points by passing a Frisbee across a field to an end zone.

ON THE FIELD

Newer types of plastic were not only easy to mold but also durable and easy to clean. This made them perfect for a variety of inventive new outdoor toys. David Mullany invented the Wiffle ball, a lightweight, plastic baseball substitute, in 1953. The lighter ball allowed Mullany's young son to practice throwing curveballs and other tricky pitches without tiring his arm.

On Thanksgiving 1937, Walter Morrison discovered that disc-shaped cake pans made excellent flying toys. He and his wife began selling the pans as toys at local parks. After serving in World War II (1939–1945) as a pilot, Morrison returned home and developed a molded plastic version of the discs, which he called Pluto Platters. In 1957, he sold the invention to the Wham-O toy company, who marketed it as the Frisbee.

In the early 1960s, chemist Norm Stingley discovered that a certain kind of rubber could be used to create incredibly bouncy balls. Stingley sold his invention to Wham-O, who marketed it as the Super Ball. When the Super Ball hit stores in 1965, it became an instant sensation and remained a best seller for years.

PAST MARVELS

This man is working at the original Lego workshop in the Danish city of Billund.

THE PERFECT DESIGN

Each Lego block has pegs on top and holes on the bottom so they can lock together. After the introduction of the first Lego bricks, the company slowly refined the design until it was perfected in the late 1950s. Since then, all Lego bricks have been created using the same measurements, which are planned down to the **micrometer**. This means that Lego pieces purchased today can connect just as well to Legos from 1960 as they can to modern ones!

Early Lego pieces came in a smaller range of shapes than today's pieces do.

THE LEGO LEGACY

Not all toys need modern technology or flashy new features to stay popular. Some toys are such good ideas that they remain popular for decades. In 1932, Danish carpenter Ole Kirk Christiansen founded a toy company and named it Lego, from the Danish words for "play well." At first, the company focused on wooden toys, but in 1947 it began experimenting with the new possibilities of plastic. Two years later, the first studded, interlocking Lego bricks were sold.

On average, people around the world purchase about seven Lego sets per second.

BUILDING NEW WORLDS

The 1970s saw the introduction of the first Lego "minifigures," which are small plastic characters that can interlock with Lego pieces. In the following years, Lego began to introduce a variety of themed sets, allowing kids to build models such as castles, spaceships, and trains.

Around 19 billion new Lego pieces are created each year.

NEW WAYS TO PLAY

In 1969, Lego began selling a new system of building toys that it called Duplo. Duplo pieces are much larger than regular Lego pieces, making them a better choice for small children who might swallow small items. As these children got older, they could use the smaller Lego bricks along with their Duplo pieces. This ensured that kids would not outgrow their old Lego toys.

In 1977, Lego released the first sets in its Technic system. Like Duplo pieces, Technic sets could be combined with standard Lego pieces. However, they were aimed at older children who might want to build realistic vehicles with small moving parts. ✷

READY FOR ACTION

Toy companies began selling sets of green plastic army men after World War II. They quickly became popular among young boys. War toys became even more popular in 1964, when Hasbro released G.I. Joe. The original G.I. Joe was very similar to a Barbie doll. It was about 12 inches (30 centimeters) tall and could be outfitted with removable uniforms and accessories. The creators at Hasbro did not think boys would want to play with something called a doll, so they called G.I. Joe an "action figure." It was the first of its kind.

In the following years, toy companies began making smaller action figures made entirely of plastic, with no removable clothing. These figures became a sensation in 1977, when Kenner released a series of toys based on the movie *Star Wars*. Doll-like action figures were no longer popular, and Hasbro soon redesigned G.I. Joe to be more like the *Star Wars* toys.

MODERN G.I. JOE FIGURE

ORIGINAL G.I. JOE FIGURE

12 INCHES (30 CM) TALL

3.75 INCHES (9.5 CM) TALL

UNIFORM IS PART OF THE FIGURE'S MOLDED SHAPE

CHANGEABLE UNIFORM

ROAD WARRIORS

Young kids have long been fascinated with cars and trucks. In the 1950s, the British company Lesney Products began to sell small die-cast metal vehicles. The toys were known as Matchbox cars because their packaging looked like the boxes that matches came in.

In the late 1940s and early 1950s, Mound Metalcraft of Minnesota manufactured a variety of household metal goods. But the business really took off in the mid-1950s when it changed its name to Tonka Toys and began producing die-cast toys. The company's sturdy yellow dump trucks and other construction vehicles became its most famous products.

Mattel launched its Hot Wheels line in 1968. Fake rubber wheels made the toys roll faster than any other die-cast vehicles. Hot Wheels also came with eye-catching paint jobs and crazy features such as oversized engines.

Die-cast toys, such as this Matchbox car, are made of durable molded metal.

More than 4 billion Hot Wheels cars have been produced since 1968.

Ty Inc. created more than 1,700 different Beanie Babies.

FUZZY FRIENDS

Always popular, huggable plush toys became bigger than ever in the 1980s and 1990s. Xavier Roberts, a college student, designed the large-headed Cabbage Patch Kids in 1978. The plush dolls reached stores four years later and began selling at an incredible rate. Roberts's creations were so popular that parents were forced to search frantically through sold-out stores to find the dolls at Christmastime.

Former plush toy salesman Ty Warner launched the Beanie Babies in 1993. Each "Beanie" was part plush toy and part beanbag. Warner's company, Ty Inc., steadily introduced new Beanies while retiring older models. This created a demand among collectors, as people combed toy store shelves for rare and valuable Beanies.

Tickle Me Elmo, a talking plush doll based on the popular Sesame Street character Elmo, was in such high demand near Christmas of 1996 that shoppers sometimes fought each other while trying to purchase it!

AMAZING ART TOOLS

Art toys have gone through many changes since the crayons and finger paint that were popular in the early 1900s. In the 1950s, French electrician André Cassagnes combined glass and aluminum powder to create a new kind of drawing toy. Users could twist knobs to etch a design in the aluminum powder behind the glass, then shake it up to erase their drawings and start over. Cassagnes called it Telecran, but it became famous when the Ohio Art Company released it as the Etch-A-Sketch.

In the 1960s, British **engineer** Denys Fisher used one toy to create another when he built the Spirograph from Meccano building kits. Using a Spirograph, artists can easily draw a variety of highly complex curved designs.

Hasbro's Lite-Brite, introduced in 1967, allowed children to create pictures by placing colored plastic pegs into a light box. When the box was turned on, a lightbulb inside caused the colored pegs to shine brightly.

André Cassagnes originally named his invention L'Ecran Magique, or "The Magic Screen."

In 2010, an official Lite-Brite app was released for the iPhone and iPad, allowing users to create classic Lite-Brite designs using their touch screens.

Many of today's toys are built using the latest robotics and computer technology.

2

TODAY'S TOP TOYS

Some things never change. Kids today still play with dolls, yo-yos, blocks, and countless other toys that are popular even decades after they were introduced. At the same time, toy designers are always hard at work looking for new ways to have fun. They might invent something new simply by tweaking an old classic. Other times, a toy designer will come up with an idea so fresh that no one could have predicted it.

Today's most popular toys allow kids to explore virtual worlds and take advantage of the latest technology. The lines between computers and toys are starting to blur as designers search for new ways to make their products more interactive.

HIGH TECH TOYS

2009	2009	2011	2012
Robotic Zhu Zhu Pets become one of the latest "smart toys" to catch on with kids.	Lego releases Mindstorms NXT 2.0, its latest robotic building system.	Skylanders lets video game players bring their action figures into a virtual world.	Mattel's Apptivity toys let kids use special action figures and toy cars to play games on iPad tablets.

GET SMART

Have you ever wanted your own robot? In the 1970s, the invention of inexpensive **microprocessors** opened the door for robotic "smart toys." A smart toy is equipped with electronics that allow it to respond to its environment. Some smart toys can learn basic tasks and interact with their owners through voice and facial expressions.

Earlier smart toys, such as 1985's Teddy Ruxpin and 1998's Furby, could speak and move their faces, but not do much else. Today's smart toys are much more advanced. In 2005, the WowWee toy company released a small robot called RoboSapien. Designed by physicist Mark Tilden, the robot can be programmed to walk, talk, and even pick up and throw small objects.

In 2009, Russ Hornsby's Zhu Zhu Pets became one of the latest smart toy crazes. These small plush hamsters walk around and act like real pet hamsters.

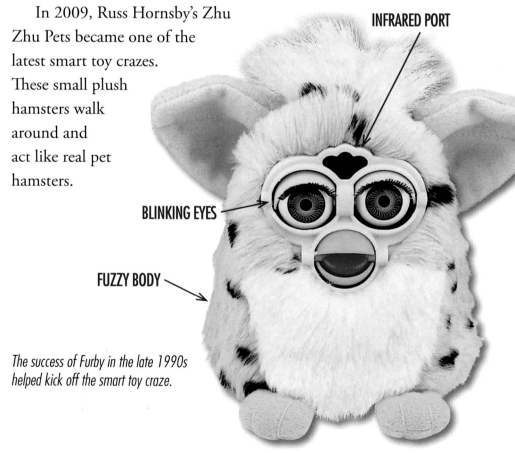

INFRARED PORT

BLINKING EYES

FUZZY BODY

The success of Furby in the late 1990s helped kick off the smart toy craze.

Mattel's Apptivity toys combine popular toys such as Hot Wheels with iPad activities and games.

iTOYS

Though it once seemed like something out of a science fiction movie, it is normal today to see someone pull a smartphone or tablet computer from his or her pocket and use it to perform some convenient function. Toys makers are taking advantage of this technology with some of their latest designs. Mattel's Apptivity toys interact with iPad apps to let kids play a variety of fun games. These toy cars and figures are equipped with special sensors that allow them to interact with the tablet's touch screen. Hot Wheels Apptivity cars are one of the most popular options. Kids can race these classic die-cast cars along a variety of virtual tracks.

Even the youngest kids are getting a chance to enjoy smartphones and tablets. Fisher-Price's Apptivity Monkey allows parents to secure an iPhone inside a soft, colorful monkey. Babies and small children can use the touch screen for fun learning activities, and the expensive electronic device is kept safe from possible damage.

FROM THIS TO THAT

DRIP, DRIP, DRIP

Water guns date back to the end of the 1800s. These early squirt guns consisted of a tube, a squeezable bulb, and a gun-shaped toy. When kids squeezed the bulbs, it pushed water through the tube and out of the gun. Later squirt guns were able to eliminate the bulb and tube by taking advantage of the same technology that makes spray bottles work. Kids could simply pull the squirt gun's trigger to fire it. The earliest versions of these squirt guns were made of metal, but plastic ones became more common in the mid-1900s.

Squirt gun technology has improved greatly over time.

THE WETTEST WEAPONS

It can be tough to cool down on a hot day. One great way to beat the heat is a water fight. For decades, kids have been tossing water balloons, spraying each other with hoses, and, best of all, blasting each other with squirt guns.

Simple plastic squirt guns do not hold a lot of water and cannot squirt very far.

Water bazookas are usually used in pools or at beaches.

BLASTING WITH BAZOOKAS

Water bazookas take a slightly different approach to summertime water combat. These plastic water guns are perfect for pools or beaches. Users stick one end of the gun underwater and then pull out the back end to suck in water. When the back is pressed in, a jet of water launches out the front of the bazooka to soak everything in its path.

ARMS RACE

Squirt gun technology underwent a huge change in 1989 when inventor Lonnie Johnson created the Super Soaker. Johnson was known for his engineering work on important space projects for NASA, but at home he tinkered with other inventions for fun. While working on one of these home projects, Johnson found that an air pump could blast water from a hose at high speed. He applied the technology to a high-powered squirt gun. Johnson sold the Super Soaker plans to Larami toys, and the squirt guns hit stores in 1990. Since then, more than 200 million Super Soakers have been sold. ✳

Air-powered squirt guns can squirt a focused jet of water.

TREMENDOUS TABLETS

Many toy companies are making tablet computers that are just for kids. They are made of durable plastic and cost far less than most other tablets. This makes them a good choice for small children who might damage a more expensive device. Just like iPads or Android tablets, LeapFrog's LeapPad and VTech's Innopad devices feature a touch screen, a microphone, and a built-in video camera. Kids can use the tablets to play games, listen to music, watch videos, and read interactive e-books.

The MEEP! tablet, by Oregon Scientific, is designed for slightly older kids. It is an actual Android tablet that can connect to the Internet and download a variety of fun and educational apps. Users can even buy accessories such as a drum pad or a keyboard to compose their own music.

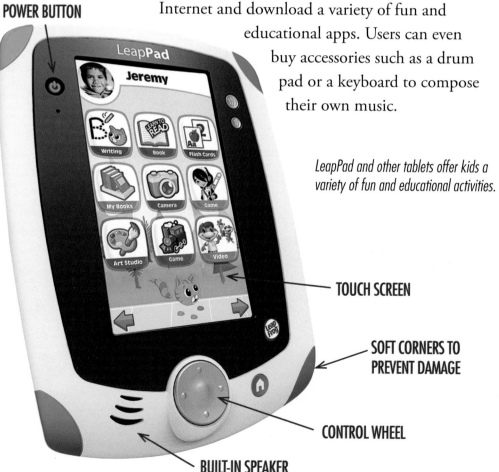

POWER BUTTON

LeapPad and other tablets offer kids a variety of fun and educational activities.

TOUCH SCREEN

SOFT CORNERS TO PREVENT DAMAGE

CONTROL WHEEL

BUILT-IN SPEAKER

CUTTING-EDGE CLASSICS

Since their debuts decades ago, Lego blocks and Barbie dolls have remained among the most successful toys in the world. But that doesn't mean that they haven't changed at all. In 1998, Lego introduced a new line of programmable robotic pieces called Mindstorms. Users can build robots using Lego pieces, then program them to perform a variety of actions. The latest version, called Lego Mindstorms NXT 2.0, was released in 2009. It contains special Lego pieces that can sense touch, motion, and color, and it also has several different motors. Users can combine these pieces with standard Lego pieces to create their own incredible robots.

One of Mattel's most recent Barbie creations is the Barbie Photo Fashion doll. This Barbie wears a special T-shirt with an LCD screen built into it. Users can plug the doll into their computers to create new graphics that display right on Barbie's T-shirt.

SENSOR EYES

PROGRAMMABLE MINDSTORMS COMPUTER AND MOTOR

GEARS FOR LEG MOVEMENT

Lego Mindstorms allow users to build their own robots and program them to perform complex actions.

MODERN MARVEL

TAKE TO THE SKIES

Action figures and video games collided like never before with the 2011 release of *Skylanders: Spyro's Adventure. Skylanders* is an action-packed video game that lets players control characters based on collectible action figures. Each action figure contains a special computer chip. When the figure is placed on a "portal" attached to the video game system, the character appears in the game for the player to control. Each character has different in-game abilities, allowing players to get a new game experience with each action figure.

BUILDING CHARACTER

As players battle enemies in the virtual *Skylanders* world, their characters earn gold and upgrades for their abilities. They also grow more powerful. All of this progress is stored on the action figure's computer chip. If the player reaches a tough part of the game with one of the characters, he or she can switch to one of the stronger action figures.

Skylanders characters appear in the video game world when they are placed on the Portal of Power.

Skylanders games have been released for several video game consoles, including the PlayStation 3, Wii, Xbox 360, and Nintendo 3DS.

ON THE GO

Because each character's progress is stored inside the action figure, players can take their favorite characters along for the ride when they go to visit friends. Two players can join forces with their own figures to battle computer-controlled enemies. They can also go head-to-head in a competition to see who has the stronger character.

CRAZY COLLECTORS

Skylanders fans go crazy for the game's collectible figures. When new characters are released, toy stores are often swarmed with fans who want to get the latest models. Some figures are more difficult to find than others, and some are only available at certain stores. This makes finding the new toys a game of its own! In 2012, a sequel called *Skylanders: Giants* was released. Of course, the new game also saw the release of new action figures, once again driving fans into a frenzy to find their favorites on toy store shelves. ☀

Fans have purchased more than 100 million Skylanders figures since the series launched in 2011.

THE NEW GIRLS IN TOWN

Barbie has long been one of the most popular dolls around, but she isn't the only girl that kids want to hang out with these days. The first three American Girl dolls were made available in 1986, and their popularity has grown incredibly ever since. The dolls were originally created to teach girls about different periods of American history. Each doll came with a life story and clothing to reflect the time period she came from. Later, dolls with modern clothing were introduced, making the line more popular than ever. Today, millions of girls flock to American Girl Place stores, where they can purchase clothing, furniture, and other accessories for their dolls. By 2008, American Girl dolls were among the most popular toys in the United States.

MATCHING OUTFITS

DOLL-SIZED TEACUP

American Girl Place stores feature restaurants where doll owners can dine with their dolls.

PLEASANT ROWLAND

American Girl dolls were created by educator Pleasant Rowland. Rowland hoped that the dolls would encourage kids to learn about history. After her huge success with American Girl, Rowland sold the company in 2000. Since then, she has devoted herself to **philanthropy**.

ROBOTS IN DISGUISE

Have you ever stood in a toy store, trying to decide between two different toys? Should you get a truck or an action figure? An airplane or a helicopter? Transformers make choices like these much easier. They are two toys in one!

Originally introduced in 1984, Transformers are some of the most famous toys ever created. Each one is a robot action figure that folds up to form a different object. Some transform into vehicles, while others take the shape of animals. Unlike other action figures, they vary widely in size. Some are only a few inches tall, while others are several times larger. Transformers became more popular than ever in 2007, with the release of a hit movie based on the characters. The toys have also inspired comic books and cartoons, and thousands of fans come together every year for conventions where they can meet the toys' creators and trade rare Transformers.

New Transformers toys based on the movie Transformers: Dark of the Moon *were released in 2011.*

31

Toy inventor Michael McGinnis showed off his 3D maze, Perplexus, at Toy Fair 2010. Toy inventors bring their creations to Toy Fair events in the hope that they will gain attention and become popular hits.

CHAPTER THREE

ON THE JOB

It is not easy to succeed in the toy industry. Creating the next big thing takes a combination of creativity, hard work, and pure luck. In many other industries, consumers are always looking for the latest and greatest new things. Most people would rather play the latest video games than classics from years past. When people buy computers, they try to get the newest, fastest ones they can afford. But with toys, many of the biggest sellers are the same types of things that people have been playing with for years. Very few new toys reach the same heights of popularity. Sometimes a toy designer might have a great idea, but it might not catch on among toy buyers. To prevent this from happening, toy makers put a lot of hard work into every new creation.

DARING DOLLS

1890	1959	1986	2010
Inventor Thomas Edison begins selling the world's first talking dolls.	Barbie is released, popularizing dolls that are shaped like adults instead of babies.	The first American Girl dolls are released exclusively through the company's catalog.	Mattel introduces its Monster High dolls, which feature designs based on popular movie monsters.

Engineering classes provide students with the skills they will need to create tomorrow's most amazing innovations.

AN EDUCATION IN ENGINEERING

Very few universities have programs for designing toys. Some art schools offer classes on toy design, but students cannot pursue full degrees in the subject. Instead, virtually all future toy makers enroll in engineering programs when they go to college. Engineering is the process of designing and building things. Different branches of the field specialize in different aspects of this process. However, all engineers have some background in science and math. They learn how to solve problems and use a variety of tools and materials. These skills come in handy when building the next hit toy.

FROM DREAM TO DESIGN

Before a team of engineers can build a new toy, they need an idea to work from. New ideas come from toy designers. Designers rely on creativity to be successful. They are always thinking about possibilities for new toys or ways to improve older versions of toys. Sometimes they join forces with other designers to brainstorm ideas. Once a designer has a good idea, he or she sketches out a rough illustration of what the product might look like. Sometimes the designer draws these plans by hand. Other times, he or she uses computer software to create 3D models. These early drafts are the first step on the road to creating a toy kids will love.

Toy designers often use computers to develop their ideas for new products.

AN INTERVIEW WITH TOY DESIGNER NATE LAU

Nate Lau is a toy designer at Tegu, a company that creates magnetic wooden block toys. Tegu uses tropical hardwood from the nation of Honduras and plants trees to replace the ones that are cut down for use in its toys. Its blocks are designed to have shapes that encourage creativity in kids.

When did you realize you wanted to design toys? For as long as I can remember, I have enjoyed drawing and could often be found with a pencil in hand. Little sketches of planes or cars and sometimes just completely random doodles would find their way onto the margins of my homework, my tests, and even my desks at school. Who would have thought those doodles would end up becoming a real thing?

What kinds of things did you study or work on to prepare for your career? At first I pursued a career in architecture but soon realized that the gigantic scale of the projects was a little overwhelming. I preferred to work on things that I could hold in my hands, and product design allows you to do that. Although I'm in toy design right now, a toy is just a specialized type of product. I never thought I'd be working for a toy company when I was growing up, but it all started with my love for drawing!

Are you ever surprised by how children apply their own ideas to your toys? We love seeing kids play with our blocks. I'm never surprised by what they come up with, because I expect kids to be wild and creative! That's what kids do best!

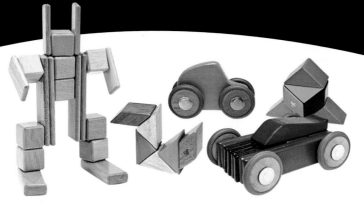

Once you have an idea for a new toy, what factors must you consider before you move forward? Tegu's purpose is to be known for excellent products that make sense while being beautifully designed. We have also made a commitment to supporting the country of Honduras and its environment by locating our factory there, creating jobs, and **repopulating** the forest. And, of course, there's our goal of utilizing new and old materials to be as environmentally **sustainable** as possible.

It takes an entire team to bring a toy from idea to completion. Does working as part of a team come naturally to you, or was it something you had to learn? When you spend your childhood hunched over a piece of paper with a pencil in hand, you don't gain many useful skills for working in a team. The good news is that design school has a way of opening your eyes and ears to other opinions and making it second nature to seek out additional views from people like you, and people who are completely different.

As an adult, how do you get yourself to think like a child while still keeping the technical side of your job in mind? I think when you become a professional designer, the difficulty comes in reminding yourself that it's OK to be a kid at times. Accessing the inner child is no problem as long as you remember that it's alright, and even encouraged.

Do you have an idea for your ultimate toy? What would you create if you had all the time and resources in the world? Now that Tegu offers magnetic wheels so kids can build their own cars to their own design with a simple pull and click, I think about how awesome it would be if there was a full-sized version to build your own pedal car or soapbox racer and customize it to your liking.

What advice would you give to a young person who wants to design toys one day? Keep drawing, anything, anywhere. Practice really does make perfect, but it won't seem like practice if it's something you enjoy. Nobody said work can't be fun. ✷

INVENTING THE INGREDIENTS

Take a look at the objects around you. Every item made by humans is made up of a variety of raw materials. Your clothes might be made of cotton or wool. This book was made using paper. More complicated items like toys might be made using a number of different materials, such as plastics, metals, or woods. Each material has its own particular strengths and weaknesses. Some plastics are more flexible than others, for instance, and some metals are easier to mold into small shapes.

Materials engineers are in charge of creating and choosing these materials. Sometimes they create brand new types of plastic for more durable toys. Other times, they might look for a metal that is just the right hardness for a certain project. They also create new methods for molding materials into different shapes, and test the materials in toys to be sure they are not poisonous or otherwise harmful. A strong background in chemistry and physics gives them the knowledge they need to excel.

A materials engineer might examine many different kinds of plastic before choosing the right one for a certain toy.

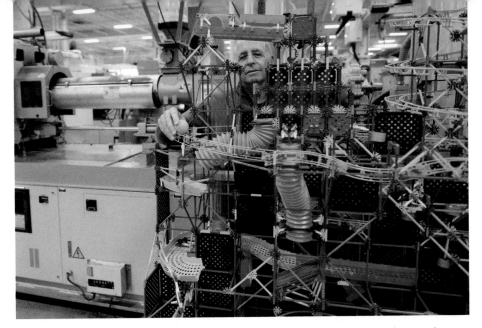

K'NEX inventor Joel Glickman relied on careful planning and engineering to create his complex building toys.

MAKING MOVEMENT WORK

Some of today's most popular toys are complex mechanical devices. They are made up of many small, moving parts, and often rely on motors or other internal mechanisms to work properly. It is up to mechanical engineers to ensure that a toy's many components all work together properly.

During the development process, mechanical engineers analyze the toy's design and decide how best to accomplish the team's goals. For example, a designer might want an action figure's arms to move in a certain way when a button on the toy's back is pressed. Mechanical engineers examine the shape of the toy and design a mechanism that will produce the arm motion the designer had in mind. If a designer wants to build a toy airplane that glides when someone throws it, mechanical engineers use their knowledge of physics to figure out how the plane should be shaped and how heavy it should be. Problem solving is the name of the game for these clever creators.

THE ARTISTIC SIDE

THE POWER OF PACKAGING

When it comes to selling big in the toy industry, a toy's packaging is almost as important as the toy itself. Artists and **marketing** experts work together to create boxes, wrappers, and other types of packaging that will capture the attention of kids and parents alike.

FINDING AN AUDIENCE

Toy packaging serves several purposes, but the most important one is drawing in customers. Artists use packaging to make a toy look as fun and exciting as possible. They include images of the toy in action, along with bright colors and exciting phrases.

Plastic toy packaging allows customers to get a look at the product while ensuring that small pieces are not lost or damaged on the way to store shelves.

They also try to make sure the packaging will appeal to the types of people they think will buy the toy. For example, the boxes that Barbie dolls come in are often bright shades of pink and purple, which are likely to draw in young girls. When packaging features photos of children using the toys, designers must make sure that the kids in the photos are around the same age as the kids who will buy the toy. Older kids won't want a toy if they think it is made for babies!

Stuffed animals are often sold in packages that allow shoppers to feel the toys before purchasing them.

HANDS ON

Many toy packages give potential customers a chance to take some of the toy's most impressive features for a test-drive. Small holes might let kids reach a finger inside to press a button and hear the toy talk. Many dolls come in packaging that leaves almost the entire toy open to touch. Getting to see and handle the toy up close can encourage people to buy it.

TO THWART A THIEF

Toy packaging is also designed to help prevent people from stealing the toys from stores. One way to avoid theft is to put small toys in large packages. For example, action figures and die-cast cars are often very small. A thief could easily put them in his or her pocket and leave the store. But most of these small toys are encased in a type of packaging known as a blister pack or clamshell packaging. This is a small bubble of plastic that is attached to a larger piece of cardboard. Because the cardboard is large, the toy is more difficult to steal. It also gives artists more room for eye-catching designs! ✳

Blister packs make small toys more difficult for thieves to place in their pockets or purses.

Many modern toys are packed with computer chips and other electronic components.

TOY TECHNOLOGY

Because so many modern toys are built using computer technology and electronic devices, computer and electrical engineers have come to play a major role at many toy companies. Computer engineers understand the ins and outs of designing and building computer systems using a variety of hardware components. If a toy has any sort of microchip or more complex computer system inside, a computer engineer likely designed it.

Electrical engineers specialize in electricity and power sources. They play a role in creating even the simplest electronic toys. For example, an electrical engineer might design the system that powers a battery-operated robot or a rechargeable tablet computer.

PROGRAMMING PLAYTHINGS

Computer hardware doesn't do much good if there is no software to control it. Software engineers and programmers work together to create the programs that tell a toy's hardware what to do. Software engineers begin by determining what kind of computer program the toy needs. They then create a plan for building that software. One way they do this is by creating flowcharts to illustrate the various functions the software will need to perform in different situations.

If the toy company has a separate team of programmers, the engineer will provide them with a plan and supervise as they write the code using a computer language. At other companies, software engineers do the programming themselves.

This shape is called a terminator. It is used to mark the first and last steps of a process.

Rectangles are used to represent steps of a process.

Diamonds are used to indicate decision points.

Yes

No

This would be the step taken if the decision was "yes."

This would be the step taken if the decision was "no."

An answer of "no" could lead to an extra step before the process is complete.

Another terminator shape marks the end of the chart.

Flowcharts use a variety of shapes to outline the steps in a complex process. Here is an example of a very simple flowchart.

BRIGHT COLORS ATTRACT SHOPPERS' ATTENTION.

SALESPEOPLE HELP ANSWER CUSTOMERS' QUESTIONS.

WIDE AISLES GIVE KIDS PLENTY OF ROOM TO MOVE AROUND AND LOOK AT THE TOYS.

ENDCAPS OFFER THE MOST VISIBILITY TO SHOPPERS.

Similar toys are grouped together at toy stores, with the latest and most popular playthings placed at the end of aisles, where they are most easily seen.

CHAPTER FOUR

A TOY'S TIMELINE

The toy industry can be extremely competitive, with companies constantly battling for toy buyers' attention and money. As soon as one toy company has a hit on its hands, others rush to catch up and release similar toys in order to take advantage of the trend. This high level of competition from rival companies pressures toy makers to get their product out on time. As one Hasbro executive put it, "In this business, if you're not there first, you're not there."

Toy creators get to see their work come together quickly. A product goes from the idea stage to store shelves in 6 to 12 months. Toy companies call this period time to market. A design that lands on an engineer's desk in July may be the hit toy of the next holiday season.

LEGENDARY TOY STORES

1760	1870	1948	1992
Hamleys toy store is founded in London, England.	Frederick August Otto Schwarz opens the shop that will eventually become the world famous FAO Schwarz toy store.	Charles P. Lazarus opens Children's Bargain Town, which is later renamed Toys"R"Us.	The first Lego retail store is opened at the Mall of America in Bloomington, Minnesota.

Toy designers might present their ideas to coworkers using drawings or charts.

GOOD IDEAS

All toys begin with an idea. Where that idea comes from, however, can be very different depending on the type of toy being created and what kinds of companies are involved. Sometimes it might be as simple as a designer having a sudden inspiration for a brand-new product. Other times, toy company executives might ask a team of designers to improve one of their old products or create new toys based on an upcoming movie.

Once designers put together rough plans for a new toy, they must seek approval before moving forward. A design team at the toy giants Mattel or Hasbro has to impress decision makers inside the company. Designers at a company that makes toys for fast-food kids' meals or cereal boxes, on the other hand, must please the clients who have hired them.

Other toy designers are independent and do not have to answer to anyone. They come up with a unique idea and then move forward with the project on their own. This is how such legendary toys as Super Soakers and Beanie Babies were created.

PLAYING WITH PROTOTYPES

Once a design is approved, toy makers must turn their rough drawings into a physical object. This first version of a toy is known as a **prototype**. A prototype is a functioning model of the toy, but it is far from a final product. It is usually built using whatever materials happen to be available. Scraps from previous toy designs, spare computer parts, and homemade pieces can all be found in early prototypes. Designers and engineers can use these early models to quickly see whether or not certain planned features will work. If there are major problems, the team might have to make some adjustments or even start over from scratch.

A prototype of an action figure might be uncolored or lack other details that the final product will have.

WHERE THE MAGIC HAPPENS

Professor David Wallace (right) is one of the instructors of the Toy Product Design class at MIT.

TOY SCHOOL

The Massachusetts Institute of Technology (MIT) in Cambridge, Massachusetts, and the University of Minnesota (UMN) in Minneapolis, Minnesota, are two of the many schools that are training tomorrow's toy makers. Students who attend these two universities are able to take a class called Toy Product Design. Students enrolled in the class break up into five- or six-person teams led by mentors and instructors. Each team's goal is to design and build a toy prototype.

THE STARTING LINE

Each team must start its project from scratch. The members begin by brainstorming ideas for their toys. They think about what kinds of toys people might actually want to buy. They also consider whether they will have the time and resources to complete the project by the end of the semester. Like professional toy designers, they sketch out rough ideas on paper and then create more detailed drawings to use as **blueprints** for the prototype.

One group of students in the 2012 UMN class created a toy called Stack Track. Wooden blocks can be stacked to create winding pathways for marbles.

PUTTING IT TOGETHER

Once the team members have settled on an idea and drawn up plans, they can begin the process of actually building their toy. Because they are all engineering students, they have the background knowledge they need in order to select materials, solve problems, take measurements, and assemble a working toy. If they run into especially difficult issues, they can consult their instructors for guidance.

THE BIG SHOW

By the end of the semester, each team must have a working prototype to present. The class then holds an event known as PLAYsensation. There, the students' creations are shown off to professors, professional toy designers, and the most important critics of all—children!

TONS OF TOYS

The toys shown off at PLAYsensation events are often very impressive. Students have built everything from a motorized skateboard to a remote control pirate boat with a built-in water cannon. Other students have designed art toys, musical instruments, and unique stuffed animals. ✳

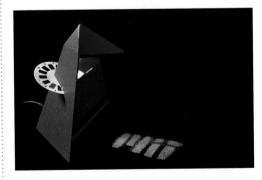

Students in the 2009 MIT class created a device that projects instructions for folding origami onto pieces of paper.

During play testing, toy designers watch to see how kids react to new toy designs.

TAKING TOYS FOR A TEST-DRIVE

Once the toy makers are confident that their prototype will work, the toy can move along in the production process. The company's testing department invites groups of children to try out its prototypes in a fun atmosphere. Specially trained employees observe the playgroups to keep an eye on how the children play with the toy. The company wants to see if children play with the toy in the way the designers planned and if they can figure out how to play with the toy without instructions. The toy must also fill its intended role. Educational toys must teach, while art toys should encourage children to be creative in fun ways.

DECISION TIME

Once a prototype has been play tested, the toy company's research and development (R&D) department judges whether it should be turned into a finished toy. If the playgroups did not play with the toy the right way or if they didn't have fun with it, the team might have to make some changes or even scrap the project.

The company also takes other issues into account when deciding whether or not to move forward with a project. They experiment with different ways to manufacture the toy and estimate how much it will cost to produce. They then weigh this information against an estimate of how popular they expect the toy to be. If they believe that the toy will be profitable, engineers can start on a final plan for the product.

Research and development departments examine prototypes to determine whether the company should manufacture a toy.

Engineers examine every detail of a new toy to look for possible flaws.

DOWN TO THE DETAILS

Once the toy company's engineers receive the go-ahead to work on a promising toy idea, they begin experimenting and looking for ways to make a fun and durable product while keeping manufacturing costs as low as possible. Different kinds of engineers work on different kinds of toys.

Much of the engineers' work takes place on computers. Special software allows them to experiment with different parts and materials without actually building a toy. For example, they can run simulations to see if a certain part will hold up against stress or snap in two. Each part is examined over and over again to make sure it can be manufactured easily and inexpensively. In addition, a part must hold up through years of play.

REDUCING RISKS

Safety is an important issue when designing toys. This is especially true for toys made for younger children. Engineers must take many factors into account when testing toy designs for safety. They must consider every possibility for injury. Does the toy have sharp pieces that can cut kids? Are there moving parts that could trap fingers or hair? Special software allows engineers to determine whether a toy will shatter if pounded on a table or if it could possibly suffocate a child. Every company has a program that simulates a child's throat to make sure no single part can be swallowed or cause the child to choke. For example, small holes were added to the plastic heads of Lego minifigures in recent years. These holes allow a child to continue breathing if he or she accidentally gets one of the plastic heads stuck in his or her throat. Engineers also ensure that none of the toy's materials are poisonous, in case a child puts the toy in his or her mouth.

Toys that break easily can pose a threat to young children who might injure themselves on the broken parts.

LASTING CONTRIBUTIONS

STAYING POWER

Some kinds of toys never go out of style. Kids have been playing with simple wooden toys for thousands of years. Even with the popularization of cheap, easily moldable plastics in the 20th century, wooden toys never went away completely.

KEEPING IT SIMPLE

Some parents purchase wooden toys for their children because they believe the toys encourage creative thinking. The children can use their imaginations to turn simple block shapes into cities, castles, or alien worlds. More modern toys usually have very specific shapes, which give kids fewer options when they are playing.

The simple shapes and bright colors of wooden blocks never go out of style.

ALL NATURAL

Wooden toys are also more environmentally friendly than plastic toys. Though trees must be cut down to obtain wood, trees can be regrown. Many wooden toy companies even take responsibility for replanting trees themselves. Plastic is usually made using oil, which is a limited resource found beneath the planet's surface. The world's oil supply is limited, and it cannot be regrown when it is used.

Tegu's environmentally friendly blocks use magnets to stick together.

Replanting trees can help make up for the damage caused by harvesting wood for toys and other products.

OLD TOYS, NEW MAKERS

Large toy companies such as Mattel and Hasbro do not make many wooden toys today. Instead, parents purchase these playthings from newer, smaller companies that focus exclusively on wooden toy designs. PlanToys offers a variety of wooden animals, vehicles, and games for young children. Tegu manufactures magnetic wooden blocks that can be used to build anything a child imagines. Melissa & Doug makes everything from art toys and games to pretend tools and kitchen items. ✳

```
'resource_id'                    ➡ $role_details['id'],
);                               ➡ $resource_details['id'],
( $this->rule_exists( $resource_details['id'], $role_det
if ( $access == false ) {
    // Remove the rule as there is currently no need fo
    $details['access'] = !$access;
    $this->_sql->delete( 'acl_rules', $details );
} else {
    // Update the rule with the new access value
    $this->_sql->update( 'acl_rules', array( 'access' =
}
foreach( $this->rules as $key=>$rule ) {
    if ( $details['role_id'] == $rule['role_id'] && $de
        if ( $access == false ) {
            unset( $this->rules[ $key ] );
        } else {
            $this->rules[ $key ]['access'] = $access;
        }
    }
```

During bug testing, programmers search every line of their code for errors.

THE EXTERMINATORS

Because so many toys today rely on computers, they must be carefully
tested for bugs before they can be released. Just as with any computer
software, there can sometimes be unforeseen effects once someone
actually starts using the toy. Testers play with the toy in every way they
can possibly think of, hoping to uncover any problems that software
engineers or programmers might have missed. It is very important that
any bugs are squashed before the toy is sold to the public. If the toy has a
problem that causes it to malfunction, the company might have to **recall**
it. This is an expensive and embarrassing process, and companies do
everything they can to prevent such situations from arising.

FROM FACTORY FLOOR TO STORE SHELVES

Once every aspect of the toy has been finalized, the toy company makes plans to manufacture it in large quantities. Molds and dies are created to shape the plastic and metal pieces that will be used to build the toy, and the company's factories are prepared for the manufacturing process. This can be a long, globe-spanning process. A toy company headquartered in New York City might have a plastic mold manufacturer in Osaka, Japan, and a factory in Guangzhou, China.

Once the toys have been built and are secure inside their packaging, they are shipped to toy stores. Will the new toy be the next big thing? It is up to the parents and children of the world to decide.

Toy molds are created by cutting shapes into heavy blocks of metal.

THE FUTURE

The Google Glass device places a computer screen right in front of the user's eye. Such devices could be used to create augmented reality games and toys.

WHAT'S NEXT?

When it comes to creating new concepts and building on the success of today's favorites, toy creators aren't showing any signs of slowing down. Right this minute, there is probably a designer somewhere in the world sketching out a brand-new toy, or an engineer finding a way to make an existing toy better. While we can't ever be sure what the future will hold, here are some toy trends that are likely to have a big impact in coming years.

TOYS THAT LEARN

Interactive toys are likely to become even more popular. New toys might be able to learn their owners' language, likes, dislikes, and favorite activities, and use this information to form a unique personality.

You might also start to see more interactive educational toys in classrooms. People tend to be more focused and learn better when they are doing something they enjoy. A good interactive toy could make difficult school subjects fun for children to learn.

AUGMENTED REALITY

A groundbreaking technology called **augmented** reality (AR) promises to transform the ways people play.

AR combines real-world experiences with computer-generated information. Advertisers already use AR. Today's sports fans, for example, see AR in the form of computer-generated advertisements plastered on real-life playing fields when they watch games on TV. Video game consoles and smartphones take advantage of built-in cameras to power simple AR games.

Toy creators, meanwhile, have begun combining AR with real-world toys. The tech company Qualcomm developed a storytelling prototype using Sesame Street characters. The toys in the playset feature

Tablet computers can add animated characters and backgrounds to real-world images.

Ernie and Bert and the furniture in their house. The same figures and furniture show up on a computer screen. Ernie and Bert speak dialogue that helps guide the child through stories and activities both on the screen and with the real-life toys.

Future AR toys will go much farther. Wearable devices will eliminate the need for smartphones or computer screens. Several companies are developing glasses that display digital information for the wearer to see.

The tech company Google made a splash in 2012 with an AR headset called Google Glass. Users wear the device like a pair of eyeglasses, and information is presented through a display near one eye. Such devices will be common in the near future.

GOING GREEN

As more people come to realize the importance of keeping our planet healthy and conserving natural resources, green toys are sure to grow in popularity.

Batteries are expensive to recycle. They also contain dangerous acid. The OWI toy company has created a racing car that runs on solar energy, no batteries required. Another runs on salt water. Such alternate power sources could one day become the main energy source for electronic toys.

Other toy companies have gone green by using recycled plastic and metal. Building blocks, stackable cups, and bath toys have all gotten the recycling treatment. Toysmith even sells a kit that encourages children to collect plastic grocery bags and turn the trash into a toy monster. Many companies stuff teddy bears with recycled plastic bottles. In time, many more toys might be made from recycled materials. ✳

CAREER STATS

INDUSTRIAL DESIGNERS

MEDIAN ANNUAL SALARY (2010): $58,230

NUMBER OF JOBS (2010): 40,800

PROJECTED JOB GROWTH: 10%, about average

PROJECTED INCREASE IN JOBS 2010–2020: 4,300

REQUIRED EDUCATION: Bachelor's degree in industrial design or a related field

LICENSE/CERTIFICATION: None

MATERIALS ENGINEERS

MEDIAN ANNUAL SALARY (2010): $83,120

NUMBER OF JOBS (2010): 22,300

PROJECTED JOB GROWTH: 9%, slower than average

PROJECTED INCREASE IN JOBS 2010–2020: 1,900

REQUIRED EDUCATION: Bachelor's degree in materials science or materials engineering, or a related field

LICENSE/CERTIFICATION: Most employers require a state license, available after four years of experience; test requirements vary by state

MECHANICAL ENGINEERS

MEDIAN ANNUAL SALARY (2010): $78,160

NUMBER OF JOBS (2010): 243,200

PROJECTED JOB GROWTH: 9%, slower than average

PROJECTED INCREASE IN JOBS 2010–2020: 21,300

REQUIRED EDUCATION: Bachelor's degree

LICENSE/CERTIFICATION: State license, available after four years of experience; test requirements vary by state

Figures reported by the United States Bureau of Labor Statistics

RESOURCES

BOOKS

Cunningham, Kevin. *Toys*. Ann Arbor, MI: Cherry Lake, 2009.

Hewitt, Sally. *Toys and Games*. New York: Orchard/Watts, 2004.

Kenney, Sean. *Cool Robots*. New York: Henry Holt, 2010.

Lipkowitz, Daniel. *The Lego Book*. New York: DK Children, 2012.

Ooten, Tara. *Creating the Barbie Doll: The Ruth Handler Story*. Miami: Bluewater, 2012.

Parker, Steve. *Robots for Work and Fun*. Mankato, MN: Amicus, 2011.

FACTS FOR NOW

Visit this Scholastic Web site for more information on toys:
www.factsfornow.scholastic.com
Enter the keyword **Toys**

GLOSSARY

augmented (AWG-men-tid) added to or made larger

blueprints (BLOO-prints) models or detailed plans of action

celluloid (SELL-yuh-loyd) a type of flammable plastic that was once used to manufacture toys

die-cast (DYE-kast) made using a process in which hot liquid metal is poured into a hard steel mold called a die

engineer (en-juh-NEER) someone who is specially trained to design and build machines or large structures such as bridges and roads

marketing (MAHR-kuht-ing) the practice of advertising or promoting something so people will want to buy it

micrometer (MYE-kroh-mee-tur) one one-millionth of a meter

microprocessors (MYE-kroh-prah-ses-urz) computer chips that control the functions of electronic devices

molded (MOHL-did) shaped into a particular form

philanthropy (fuh-LAN-thruh-pee) the donation of time or money to causes and charities

prototype (PROH-tuh-tipe) the first version of an invention that tests an idea to see if it will work

recall (REE-kawl) to call back a purchased product that has a defect

repopulating (ree-PAHP-yuh-lay-ting) planting new trees to replace those that have been cut down

sustainable (suh-STAY-nuh-buhl) done in a way that can be continued and that doesn't use up natural resources

vinyl (VYE-nuhl) a flexible, waterproof, shiny plastic that is used to make toys and other products

INDEX

Page numbers in *italics* indicate illustrations.

INDEX (CONTINUED)

ABOUT THE AUTHOR

KEVIN CUNNINGHAM graduated from the University of Illinois at Urbana. He is the author of more than 60 books on history, health, disasters, and other topics. He lives near Chicago, Illinois.